DEDICATION

For

Raymond L.
Maureen M.
Ruth K.S. M.
Matilda M.M.

CONTENTS

The *End Game Law of Financial Mindset* is a reset framework that assumes the end by mapping the process. It optimizes the marketing process even before the product is created.

How many minds have at least thought of what they would do if they won a jackpot? I would say, countless. Such minds assume that happiness is only possible after the money is won.

A few, though, have a different conception. They enjoy the process that might lead to the end. They love the very idea of betting or risk-taking.

That's the idea of an end game formulation. Love the process and assume the end.

I write books, and for a long time I was fascinated by how that the process of authorship excited me more than the end result – a copy in hand or money in my bank account.

Then I began to realize that it was a pattern in nature, to enjoy, and even love, the creative process.

For example, the love-making process is

super enjoyable even though giving birth and raising up a child may be painful and a challenge, etc.

Applied to finances, the *End Game Law* dictates that we enjoy the process of earning an income and celebrating it even before we see or experience the results. The process of *thinking* about money must be as the enjoyment we get from having and using it.

Ultimately, the process must be more profitable than the result.

c.m.

END GAME LAW

"Talk, discuss, write or read about money often, you will often have it."

> Interest is garnered in familiarity. This rule is contained in the principle of osmosis – everything, eventually flows.

"If you can't afford to leave monetary inheritance to your children, at least buy 'Charles Mwewa Books' for them."

> The principle is that knowledgeable ideas are in books and the writings of the wise and the prudent.

"When Government gives you a penny, work harder to return a dollar."

Government is a resultant effort of an idea called a nation. We all contribute to it and must sustain it; not dwindle it.

"Don't ask how much money Government should give you, but how much you should give it."

> Government is a resultant effort of an idea called a nation. We all contribute to it and must sustain it; not dwindle it.

"Make money, even if it's just enough to survive on."

Don't merely depend on others; expand your potential.

"If you want to be free, make your own money."

Empower yourself to be a resource, a useful conduit towards the satisfaction of the general good.

"Fear of unknowns and money have enslaved more people to others than prisons can hold."

You will always, directly, or indirectly, answer to the one who pays or gives you money.

"It's possible to love a person's money, and
not the person themselves."

Success attracts followers, and for the
most part, that's all they follow, money,
and not the person.

"Sometimes, people erroneously think that they're following a person; they're, in fact, following their money."

Success attracts followers, and for the most part, that's all they follow, money, and not the person.

"Don't let a chance to make money pass you by."

Chances are like raindrops – they add up to a flood. Use every opportunity you get to advance yourself.

"Even if you're working for someone else, always have it as a goal to be your own boss someday."

You can't be richer than the one who employs you unless you are stealing.

"If you 'like' it, buy it."

Hopelessness is defined as looking outside of your window admiring your neighbor's farm while yours if overgrown by weeds.

"Money is currency and slippery - to get it requires skill, to hold it, even more and better skills."

Valuables must be handled with extra care and diligence.

"Pareto Principle of the Mind: 20% of what you think about is responsible for 80% of your gains. Think more."

Everything that has ever been created or invented was achieved through the use of the mind.

"Money gives power to do just about anything."

Money has an exchange advantage.

"Money changes things, including you. If you can have it, you can change how people see you."

Money has an exchange advantage.

"The promise of money is the most unpredictable event on earth. Don't plan on money you don't have."

Everyone discovers that they have an unfulfilled need when they see or have money.

"End Game Law: The process must be more profitable than the result."

Money is marketing; marketing is money.

"End Game Law: If you repeat at least three times that something is good, many people will buy it. Don't be ashamed to advertise."

Money is marketing; marketing is money.

"End Game Law: Is a game-changer - tell people what you can do for them, then use their money to do it."

Money is marketing; marketing is money.

"End Game Law: Amazon and many American businesses now use it; it may be called 'delivery on demand.'"

Money is marketing; marketing is money.

"End Game Law: Simply stated, marketing comes before production. God said it before it was so should we."

> Money is marketing; marketing is money.

"The Law of Multiplication Effect: Only that which is used can multiply."

No matter how safe and secure it is, money or talent that has been buried and is unused will not solve anyone's problems.

"Think of money as a tool, a means to an end, and not the end."

No matter how rich you were, if you didn't use your wealth to help others, you were poor.

"The Pyramid Law: Those on top do less and make more money; those at the bottom do more but make less."

Only stay at the bottom if by so doing you are serving a greater good.

"There are those who use other people to make their money, and those who are used by others to make their money."

Make your money ethically.

"Anyone with a mature brain can make money."

There is nothing more common in any society in the world than money.

"You would have wasted your life on earth if all you give are excuses why you can't make or find money."

Excuses are dreams of fools.

"The parable of talents shows us that even God is interested in profit."

Good is profit-motivated.

"It is not wrong to advertise yourself or your product or your services; people rarely buy into what they least know."

Only God looks at the heart.

"Spend time making people want to have what you have or make or are."

Only God looks at the heart.

32

"Generally, people are reluctant to spend money until they are persuaded, either by need or want."

Only God looks at the heart.

"God also runs the world like a business, those who don't use their skills and talents, He will also not reward them."

Jesus: "I must be about my Father's business..." (Luke 2:49)

"The primary purpose of Government is service, but even a little child knows that services require money."

Governing is everybody's responsibility.

"Make less contracts with Government, let Government make more contracts with you. We should not depend on government so much; government must depend on us."

Governing is everybody's responsibility.

"If one has no money, in the money economy, she has no life."

> Buying and selling started even before money was invented.

"Anything that makes money must be pursued legally."

Buying and selling started even before money was invented.

"We lose more money than we spend because we least diversify it."

Buying and selling started even before money was invented.

"If you think of only one way of making money, you may be wasting chances and opportunities."

Buying and selling started even before money was invented.

"Before you manage any government department, manage your own business well."

Governing is everybody's responsibility.

"In any nation, if Government is the largest employer, many will retire well, but the nation will expire."

Governing is everybody's responsibility.

"There is nothing like 'Government property,' there is only 'Our property.'"

Governing is everybody's responsibility.

"One golden principle of government management: Re-educate those who blunder, fire those who steal."

Governing is everybody's responsibility.

"If you think of work in Government as a means to wealth, you must become corrupt."

Governing is everybody's responsibility.

"When an individual mismanages her wealth, she goes bankrupt, so are Governments."

Governing is everybody's responsibility.

"Government must hire skilled and competent people to manage its assets; if not, the nation becomes poorer."

Governing is everybody's responsibility.

"If you work for Government, you work for a business - manage its resources well."

Governing is everybody's responsibility.

"Government is a business - it must constantly be thinking and creating ways of making profit."

Governing is everybody's responsibility.

ABOUT THE AUTHOR

Best Selling Author, Charles Mwewa (LLB; BA Law; BA Ed; LLM), is a prolific researcher, poet, novelist, lawyer, law professor and Christian apologist and intercessor. Mwewa has written no less than 73 books and counting in every genre and has exhibited his works at prestigious expos like the Ottawa International Book Expo and is the winner of the Coppa Awards for his signature publication, *Zambia: Struggles of My People.*

SELECTED BOOKS BY THIS AUTHOR

1. *ZAMBIA: Struggles of My People (First and Second Editions)*
2. *10 FINANCIAL & WEALTH ATTITUDES TO AVOID*
3. *10 STRATEGIES TO DEFEAT STRESS AND DEPRESSION: Creating an Internal Safeguard against Stress and Depression*
4. *100+ REASONS TO READ BOOKS*
5. *A CASE FOR AFRICA?S LIBERTY: The Synergistic Transformation of Africa and the West into First-World Partnerships*
6. *A PANDEMIC POETRY, COVID-19*
7. *ALLERGIC TO CORRUPTION: The Legacy of President Michael Sata of Zambia*
8. *BOOK ABOUT SOMETHING: On Ultimate Purpose*
9. *CAMPAIGN FOR AFRICA: A Provocative Crusade for the Economic and Humanitarian Decolonization of Africa*
10. *CHAMPIONS: Application of Common Sense and Biblical Motifs to Succeed in Both Worlds*
11. *CORONAVIRUS PRAYERS*
12. *HH IS THE RIGHT MAN FOR ZAMBIA: And Other Acclaimed Articles on Zambia and Africa*
13. *I BOW: 3500 Prayer Lines of Inspiration & Intercession from the Heart: Volume One*
14. *INTERUNIVERSALISM IN A NUTSHELL: For Iranian Refugee Claimants*
15. *LAW & GRACE: An Expository Study in the Rudiments of Sin and Truth*
16. *LAWS OF INFLUENCE: 7even Lessons in Transformational Leadership*

INDEX

H

L

M

N

O

P

R

S

T

W

Z

www.ingramcontent.com/pod-product-compliance
Lightning Source LLC
Chambersburg PA
CBHW071509030726
47593CB00003B/1234